Dealing with Death

Published 2021
by ELOYD DIVA

ISBN 978-1-8383889-0-4

Dealing with Death

*Once you are dead,
you are made for life*

ELOYD DIVA

For my family

TABLE OF CONTENTS

Preface

My eldest daughter was killed in a car accident a few weeks before her seventeenth birthday. It was a Wednesday evening and she had football practice, but she decided not to go, as her friend wanted her to 'go for a spin' in a new car. I had telephoned her at 6 p.m. and headed home from work, as she had told me of her revised plans. At 8 p.m. she was dead and I would never see her again.

I had arrived home about 6.45 p.m. that evening and changed into some casual clothes. It was a beautiful sunny evening and the grass needed to be cut. When the job was finished, I went back inside. I poured out a bowl of cereal, filled it with milk, and then the doorbell rang. I do not like soggy cereal, so my mood was not good heading for the door.

'Your daughter is dead…'

That's all I heard. I fell to the floor as my knees gave way and I physically could not get up from the ground. I was not a pretty sight.

The emotions that I experienced from those first few days after her death up to now, many years later, have shaped me and my family. The initial feelings of helplessness, pain, and sadness have been replaced by a wonderful sense of accomplishment, fond memories, and peace. My love for her achieved this transfer of darkness into light.

2020 will be long remembered for the significant impact caused by the Corona Virus (Covid-19) with over 2,500,000 people dying from this disease to date (and rising).

In this book, I will share with you my thoughts and feelings of how we as a society view death. We can look at death from the point of view of the person who has died and also of those left behind. We can analyse our lives to prepare for our own passing, as death is a mirror in which the entire meaning of life is reflected.

Life will never be the same without her, but her death has made me a better parent, spouse, and person overall. It has meant that I no longer have to worry about her, and I am absolutely confident that she is now watching over my family and I to keep us all safe.

Anyone who has lost a loved one needs to be able to both laugh or cry when remembering those who have slipped away. I hope this booklet will help you along your journey.

Chapter 1

Circle of Life

I would like to begin with a short exercise (this will take 20 seconds). Draw a small picture of yourself on a large piece of paper, it doesn't have to be an accurate portrait – a stick figure with your name is fine, then draw a circle around it. There can be no one else in here, as you are the most important person in your world. Then draw your closest family members just outside that circle, such as your spouse, children, and parents. Put another circle around them. Outside of that, draw your closest friends, colleagues, other family members, and so on, then a circle around them. You get the picture.

Now imagine you are dead.

It's funny the way most people love the dead.
Once you are dead, you are made for life.

—Jimi Hendrix

The hardest thing in the world to hear is that someone close to you has died. It is the finality of the event that causes the most pain. There is no changing the situation or turning back the clock. The circle has been broken forever and those outside the first ring must now deal with it.

When your time is up, your time is up. However, when the initial shock has receded – which can take years in some cases – we must again question our position. If it was an elderly parent who passed away in their sleep, then we can reflect on all of the positive things they brought to our lives and be thankful that they lived a long and happy life for the most part.

Which would you prefer: to see your loved one in agonising pain and suffering, or to see them die gently in the dead of night? Most of us would not want to see them in any form of distress, and neither would those who are feeling it. We all know we are going to die at some point, but we do not give it much thought on a day-to-day basis – and rightly so.

What causes endless heartache is watching loved ones who have been a huge part of your life effectively disintegrate in front of you. Our love for them is so strong that we would gladly swap places to take their suffering away. Of course, those who are dying do not want us to do this; they want to pass away to remove the pain for everyone. The struggle for martyrdom is alive in all of us, and it is fascinating to believe that most people would even contemplate the ultimate sacrifice for other human beings.

We only get one life. Whether you are the most powerful person in the world or born into a life of abject poverty and despair, no amount of wealth or status can grant you a second chance. We are given one chance, and it is up to each of us to try to live it with as much fulfilment and happiness as our circumstances will allow.

Armed with such knowledge, it is hard to think that most

of us would trade places with those around us who are suffering. The wish to offer such a 'gift' is a result of our inner desire to help each other. Feelings of hopelessness and guilt could also be contributing factors when we are faced with such a dilemma.

The right thing to do is often the hardest, and we should not give such thoughts too much consideration. Better to comfort those who are passing before our eyes, than to add to their journey while they wait for the final curtain. You must put yourself in their shoes and imagine the same hopelessness and guilt in them that you may be feeling. Let them go, as you would want your loved ones to do with you some day.

**When God took you back, he said,
'Hallelujah, you are home.'**

—Ed Sheeran

All too often, it is the manner in which a person dies that determines the grieving process. Take for example a person who has died by suicide. Close family members and friends invariably feel guilty for not 'seeing the signs' or doing enough. But the person who died by suicide went to great lengths to cover up the truth from those closest to them. Acknowledging that they had a problem would only exacerbate the situation, as they saw it, thereby increasing the anxiety and making them feel even more distressed.

We must recognise that suicidal depression is an illness, similar to other major causes of death, such as cancer, stroke, and heart attack. The state of mind in which a person can find themselves, to give them the strength to do such an act, is what actually causes the death – not the particular way that it happens.

In effect, the person's control function has been overtaken

by another power, akin to a puppet being controlled by its master who pulls and drops its strings. The puppet itself is powerless in its movements and obeys its master irrespective of the consequences of its actions.

We may be better served to recognise that we just did not catch the illness in time, or that it was always going to be one step ahead of us. Feelings of guilt and regret need to be replaced by sadness and memories. Remember the person before the disease took hold of their body and mind, and commit to thinking about them and all the good and happiness that they brought to your life. Such feelings will allow you to acknowledge the cause instead of the 'what ifs', ultimately bringing comfort and peace to yourself and to those who have gone to a better place.

Sometimes we are better served by accepting the act than questioning its logic or rationale. What is done cannot be undone when it comes to death, and accepting it will greatly help you to deal with it. By letting go of the 'why-ing', we can move on to the crying.

Take another example: A person is involved in a car collision and dies. A car *crash* or a car *accident* – there is a big difference. A car crash, in lots of cases, could have been avoided. Drunk, suicidal, and irresponsible drivers are a substantial factor in causing collisions and the death of others. Their actions have far-reaching effects not just on families but on communities, spreading out over generations.

These types of situations require experience and highly trained personnel to deal with all sides of the equation. There are the family and friends of the victim directly involved, but also the family of the driver who caused the crash. The pain they feel is also unbearable, with shame and guilt written on their faces.

I am not saying that either side has a monopoly on who

feels the worst. The situation is unimaginable at the best of times. What I am saying is that when things like this happen, they must be faced head on by everyone concerned. Playing the blame game will not bring your loved ones back. Where someone has broken the law, then we must let the law deal with the perpetrator. It is better to pass that responsibility to those in a position to discharge the law, rather than trying to deal with this aspect of the tragedy, difficult as it is to let go. If we cannot let go of the anger, then we will not let go of the deceased.

Accidents, on the other hand, can be dealt with more easily. When someone's life is taken as a result of an accident, those left behind can grieve more easily. In this instance it can be much more difficult on the 'perpetrator', as the guilt and shame will be there from the very outset.

If you are going about your business and end up in the wrong place at the wrong time, sometimes the consequences are literally life-changing. It can mean death for one person and an emotional 'death sentence' for another. There is no positive outcome when one human being is responsible for the loss of another's life.

Forgiveness by the family of the deceased, though easier said than done, will ease the pain and suffering of the other party. A huge amount of comfort may be taken when you know or believe that your loved one's life was not taken maliciously or through neglect. Accidents do happen, and they must be seen as accidents.

Though it is difficult to put into practice, we must also accept that one day we too will fall out of the circle. I heard of a woman, Caroline, in her late sixties who was dying of terminal cancer. Her daughter would visit her in the hospice every day, and they seemed to have a happy relationship.

When her daughter left, however, Caroline would often sit

alone and cry. The reason for this was that her daughter refused to accept her mother's impending death. Instead, she spent the time encouraging her mother to 'think positively', in the hope that such thoughts would cure her mother's cancer.

This meant that Caroline had to keep her deep fears, panic, and grief to herself, with no one to share them with, no one to help her understand her life, and no one to help her find a meaning in her death.

One source of solace that is often overlooked when dealing with someone's death is the knowledge that when they are gone, they will never have to face any of the trials and tribulations of life. How would you feel if you had to watch your loved one spend the rest of their days and nights confined to a hospital bed, being fed from a tube and communicating only with their finger?

This, I believe, is worse than death itself. The hopelessness of watching an energetic and healthy body transform into that of a withering vegetable must be almost impossible to deal with. You hope that a miraculous recovery will somehow intervene, but in the end that hope can kill your spirit. Watching and participating in the slow deterioration of a loved one can erode you and your family, and there may even come a time when you think the unimaginable: they would be better off dead.

It's always quiet when there is no one around as one of our angels hits the ground.

—Bono, U2.

Chapter 2

Hide and Seek

Hide and seek is my eight-year-old's favourite game. I count to twenty and she hides. I find her and she laughs. Then it's her turn. Repeat the game for as long as the curtains remain on the wall (always a good hiding place), and you are assured of one of life's simple and rewarding pleasures.

We play hide and seek throughout our lives. There we are doing the grocery shopping when we spot someone we have not seen in a while. A feeling of inferiority takes over our body and we instinctively go for cover. We hide in the frozen-food section until the danger passes; we may even consider not doing our shopping there ever again.

This type of behaviour is perfectly normal and for the most part acceptable. In the main we are in charge of our own destiny, and if we do not want to meet someone who makes us feel uncomfortable, then I see no reason why we cannot be greedy about our own selves and who we share our time with.

We should not take such actions, however, when dealing with people who have suffered the loss of a loved one. Do not avoid them out of discomfort, embarrassment, or a fear of upsetting them. They may believe you do not care enough to sympathise with them. It is also unhelpful to recount stories of your own loss, even if your loss is triggered when you talk to a bereaved person, as this form of comfort rarely helps.

Express your sympathy in a simple but meaningful manner. Avoid using clichés such as 'Don't worry, you will meet someone else' or 'It was for the best.' These will only add to the feelings of anger and hurt in those who are bereaved.

Words of comfort such as 'I am so sorry' or 'I will say a prayer for you and you will be in my thoughts' are much more helpful and appropriate. Remember, there are no words that will take away the pain of those who are grieving, but we certainly do not want to load them with more feelings of distress and hurt.

The power of people at a time of great sadness can never be overestimated. Having good people around you when you are trying to process a difficult moment in your life can be of tremendous benefit. Those affected by the death of a loved one are better to seek and accept help and compassion as opposed to hiding from offers of such support.

Be conscious that most people go into shock when they first hear about the death of a loved one. It is extremely difficult to absorb what has happened, and grief may begin with thoughts such as 'I can't believe they're dead' or 'It all feels like a bad dream.' This numbing sense of shock and disbelief can last days, weeks, or even months. Your friend may appear to be coping well, as life does not stop no matter what the event. But it is often in these weeks and months after the death that the full force of what has happened begins to hit them.

Everyday tasks, such as working, parenting, shopping, and paying the bills, become difficult. People who were supportive at the time of death often stop calling. While friends and neighbours resume their normal lives, bereaved people face months and years of constant reminders of their loss and of the adjustments to their lives that are now necessary.

We can help someone who is dealing with death by not assuming they are over it or have enough help already. If you are unsure how to help, just ask – but try not to make vague offers like 'Call me if you need anything.' Most people find it hard to reach out. Instead, you could make specific offers of help: 'Can I do the shopping for you?' 'Will you come for a walk with me on Tuesday?'

We should also avoid offering advice on how the bereaved person should feel or act or get on with their lives. Allow them the space to make their own decisions, and don't feel offended if offers of help are refused.

I heard a joke recently that went as follows:

Paul: Hello, Mark. How are you getting on?

Mark: Hi, Paul. Not great. I had a terrible dream last night and could not rest afterwards.

Paul: Oh, why not?

Mark: Well, you and I were in the dream, and you know that both of us love sport. The pitches in heaven were fantastic, and we had just reached the Cup Final. This was the game we had been waiting for all of our lives.

Paul: That seems a really positive experience. How come you couldn't sleep after that?

Mark: Well, the bad news is that you were picked as captain – and the game is on this Sunday!

It is also important to recognise that people may need different layers of support, depending on their circumstances. Most people need general support from family, friends, and colleagues. Social support to help them through the grieving process may be sufficient in lots of cases, and will happen as a matter of course throughout the period of grieving.

Some people need extra support to help them through their bereavement. This could be because of the nature of the loss – a sudden death or the death of a child, for example – or because of other circumstances in their life. This extra support can come from volunteers who themselves have been bereaved and have had specialised training in bereavement support. Help at this level can be on a one-to-one basis or in groups and can be provided for both adults and children.

People who require such support often feel unable to cope or may not have many people around them to help. Sometimes it is easier to discuss the death of a loved one with someone who is not directly connected to the deceased, as it avoids any history or preconceptions.

Voluntary bereavement support services, self-help groups, faith groups, and community groups can provide much of this type of support and can greatly benefit those who are trying to deal with death. Well-run bereavement support agencies ensure that their volunteers are carefully selected, receive ongoing training, and are supervised by professionals. They provide a listening ear to people talking about their experience and support them in finding a way through their grief.

Finally, some people require bereavement support from specialised professionals: psychologists, psychotherapists, counsellors, and doctors. This type of support is primarily aimed at people who develop complications or become stuck in their grieving process.

No experience of death is ever easy, but the circumstances

surrounding certain deaths can cause additional difficulties for those left in the waiting room of life. The type of death or the experience of multiple losses in a short period of time can leave the survivors requiring help beyond that which family and friends may be able to offer.

Other factors, such as a history of difficulty in coping with loss, or a troubled relationship with the person who died, may also require professional intervention. For some, the feeling of grief does not ease over time, and they continue to feel distress, bitterness, and an inability to re-engage with normal life. This too will require professional and experienced help.

> *Warm summer sun,*
> *Shine kindly here,*
> *Warm southern wind,*
> *Blow softly here.*
> *Green sod above,*
> *Lie light, lie light.*
> *Good night, dear heart,*
> *Good night, good night.*
> —Mark Twain

The most important thing is when to ask for help, or when to encourage those who need it to seek it out, as we may all have difficulty in looking behind that curtain.

Chapter 3

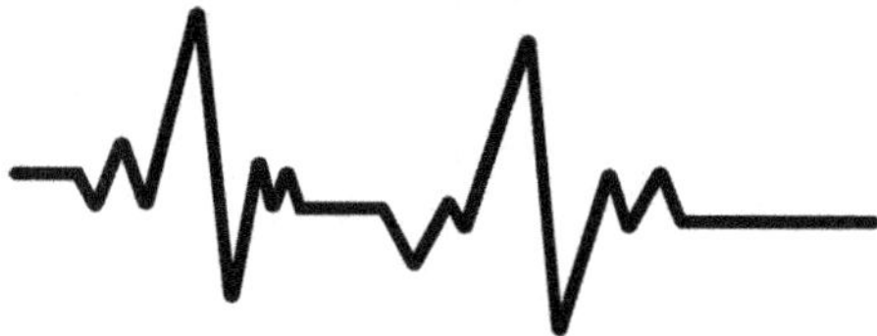

Departure Lounge

'Tom, did you put the cat out? Tom, did you hang out the washing? Tom, will you kill me? Tom, did you…'

Wait a minute, what did you say?

We all know that life is the most precious, but time-sensitive, gift that each of us possesses. We all get one spin on the merry-go-round and then it's time to get off. Some only get a few hours to enjoy it and never experience any real time on the journey, while others get to live through decades of change, entering the world with their skin as shrivelled as a dried-out prune and leaving with their skin in much the same condition.

One thing is certain for most of us: we do not know the hour or the day that our time is up. In any event we are possibly better off not being given the departure date. Written by, The Dalai Lama on the 2nd June 1992:

As a Buddhist, I view death as a normal process, a

reality that I accept will occur as long as I remain in this earthly existence. Knowing that I cannot escape it, I see no point in worrying about it. Naturally, most of us would like to die a peaceful death and so if we wish to die well, we must learn how to live well.

No less significant than preparing for our own death is helping others to die well. As a new born baby each of us was helpless and, without the care and kindness we received then, we would not have survived. Because the dying also are unable to help themselves, we should relieve them of discomfort and anxiety, and assist them, as far as we can, to die with composure.

What about those who decide they will become masters of their own destiny? Do we castigate them or scorn their decision? After all, it is their life. Are they not entitled to make that decision for themselves? Who made them God and you and I judge and jury?

Let me be clear at this juncture. I fully support the right to die, in certain circumstances. Take a situation where a person in the winter of their life is told they have been diagnosed with an incurable disease. All they can look forward to is uncertainty, pain, suffering, and the need for substantial care and attention.

Please step forward, all of my loved ones, to watch the drama unfold before you, while offering support and partaking in an ultimately fruitless exercise in medical care. My time is up, but not before I put you all through a long goodbye ritual involving doctors, nurses, neighbours, friends, and family who must watch a healthy, functioning body disintegrate daily.

For good measure, I will ensure that the show goes on for years, so you all have bad memories and can never forget the horror unfolding before you.

I imagine that in this scenario the mental torture on the

person afflicted far outweighs the physical pain they may be enduring and the impending departure date that awaits them.

As a society, are we not better served to allow our fellow citizens to decide for themselves? After all, they have lived their life to the full up to this point, contributed to society through work, taxes, volunteering, enriching the lives of others, and so on, and are now unfortunate enough to be given a ticket to leave the playground.

We could let them make up their own mind as to when they should walk out the gate, instead of leaving them to hang around waiting for it to be opened for them. Even worse: if they are not in a physical condition to be able to call time themselves, then their loved ones – whom they asked, and who absolutely, if reluctantly, agreed to help – will be treated as murderers in our criminal justice system.

Euthanasia, as defined on Wikipedia, is the practice of intentionally ending a life in order to relieve pain and suffering, or 'painless inducement of a quick death'.

The debate will depend on which side of the fence you are sitting on, of course. Advocates argue that people have a right to self-determination and thus should be allowed to choose their own destiny. Helping a person to die is more attractive than continuing to suffer. They also argue that allowing euthanasia will not lead to unacceptable consequences: in countries where it has been legalised, such as the Netherlands, Belgium, and some US states, there has been little or no negative fallout.

Those who oppose the voluntary taking of life claim that not all deaths are painful and that the use of effective pain relief can be an alternative. They often claim that the distinction between active and passive euthanasia is morally significant, and that legalising euthanasia could lead to something worse for society in the future.

Passive euthanasia is when life-sustaining treatments are withheld – but this is not as clear-cut as one may imagine. For example, if a doctor prescribes a strong painkiller that turns out to be toxic for the patient, some will argue that passive euthanasia is taking place, while others will say it is not, as there is no intention to take life.

Active euthanasia is when lethal substances or forces are applied to end a patient's life; these can be conducted by the patient themselves or somebody else. For the patient, it is important that the atmosphere around them be as peaceful as possible, and it is up to those surrounding their loved one to ensure that this happens. Active euthanasia is far more difficult for society to agree on, as individuals have moral, religious, ethical, and compassionate arguments about the issue.

Whatever the arguments for and against, I firmly believe that those of sound mind and capacity should be allowed to make their own decision. The most important thing is to avoid anything which will cause the dying person any form of distress. Our primary aim should be to help them to the gateway.

Chapter 4

Cut the Cord

I watched a film once in which a father, together with his adult son and daughter were climbing a steep mountain. One of the pins which had been driven into the side of the rock came undone, and one by one the climbers were pulled from the cliff face and left dangling mid-air, held by a single rope fastened precariously to the last remaining pin.

With the daughter at the top of the rope, the son in the middle, and their father at the bottom, things were not as they had planned when they set out that morning (it was a thriller, after all). Without a moment's hesitation, the father instructed his son to cut the rope. This would result in certain death for the father but would relieve enough pressure on the pin to save the lives of his children.

Of course, the daughter was having none of it, insisting that there had to be an alternative. But she did not know what action could save them all. The father knew that a decision had to be made and that time was of the essence. The brave son took out his knife, said goodbye to his father, and cut the lifeline, ending his father's time on this earth but saving his own life and that of his sister.

Impossible decisions are not just for the movies. They are thrust upon us all from time to time, and we must face them with courage. The consequences will have life-changing effects, but a decision has to be made. Simply ignoring the challenge at hand will not resolve the situation. Sometimes there are no fantasy lands to which to escape, no matter how much one wishes for it.

Having to decide whether you want a pregnancy to proceed or not, is one of those impossible decisions that people have faced for an eternity. There are many factors to consider, and dealing with this situation requires all of the family to show compassion to those affected.

Before challenging your viewpoint on this subject, this is what Wikipedia defines abortion as:

Abortion is the ending of pregnancy by removing a foetus or embryo before it can survive outside the uterus. An abortion that occurs spontaneously is also known as a miscarriage. An abortion may be caused purposely and is then called an induced abortion, or less frequently, 'induced miscarriage'. The word abortion is often used to mean only induced abortions. A similar procedure after the foetus could potentially survive outside the womb is known as a 'late termination of pregnancy'.

When allowed by law, abortion in the developed world is one of the safest procedures in medicine. Modern methods use medication or surgery for abortions. The drug mifepristone in combination with prostaglandin appears to be as safe and effective as surgery during the first and second trimester of pregnancy. Birth control, such as the pill or intrauterine devices, can be used immediately following abortion. When performed legally and safely, induced abortions do not increase the risk of long-term mental or physical problems. In contrast, unsafe abortions cause 47,000 deaths and millions of hospital admissions each year. The World Health Organization recommends safe and legal abortions be available to all women.

Mifepristone was first licensed for use in an abortion in France in the late 1980s. It was introduced as an alternative to surgical abortion. An editorial in the Vatican newspaper, L'Osservatore Romano, which is thought to have reflected the beliefs of Pope John Paul II, referred to the new pill as the 'pill of Cain', i.e., the monster that cynically kills its brothers.

In 1988, in the face of huge opposition from anti-abortion groups and the Catholic Church, the pharmaceutical company which produced the drug announced it would cease production. However, the then French health minister intervened and declared it the 'moral property of women' and ordered the company to continue making the drug.

About 40% of the world's women have access to legal abortions without limits as to reason. Countries that permit abortions have different limits on how late in pregnancy abortion is allowed.

For those countries that have yet to legalise abortion, they must be acutely aware that they already have abortion in their country but it is unregulated and unsafe. They continue to export their problems (i.e., women leaving for another jurisdiction for a clinical termination) and to import the solutions (i.e., women ordering pills online from India to induce abortion).

Since ancient times, abortions have been done using herbal

medicines, sharp tools, with force, or through other traditional methods. Abortion laws and cultural or religious views of abortions are different around the world. In some area's abortion is legal only in specific cases such as rape, problems with the foetus, poverty, risk to a woman's health, or incest. In many places there is much debate over the moral, ethical, and legal issues of abortion. Those who oppose abortion often maintain that an embryo or foetus is a human with a right to life and may compare abortion to murder. Those who favour the legality of abortion often hold that a woman has a right to make decisions about her own body.

Making the difficult decision to terminate a pregnancy will affect some people some of the time, some people all of the time, and possibly all of the people all of the time. It will vary with the person and the situation.

There is no turning back: only turning differently. I imagine it is something you are going to have to bring with you for the rest of your life, but with the knowledge that it was the right decision for you and your family at that time. This is the key to coming to terms with your actions. This is how you deal with this death.

From that moment on, you cannot change the act. What is done is done, and there is no time machine that will bring us back. What matters now is how we deal with it and how others around us react. The women who have had an abortion need both physical and emotional care. Family and friends have a huge role here and must be extremely conscious of what their loved ones went through. They must recognise that it is not something that can be taken care of over a hot dinner.

It is at this time that we must gather around those affected to give a helping hand. They must not be left feeling helpless or at a loss – we can provide practical and emotional support.

Remember the women's partners too, as they share the loss.

This is a marathon, not a sprint, with many hurdles thrown in to test you. Remember to enjoy yourself. You have less time left than you think.

Love can change the world in a moment, but what do I know?

—Ed Sheeran

Chapter 5

Parting Glass

"Husband slept next to his dead wife for 6 nights"
"Father takes his own life 16 months after the loss
of his 13-year-old son"

These are news headlines from around the world.

As a society we are failing to educate ourselves on how to deal with death. It is also self-evident that telephoning strangers soon after our loved ones die, to arrange the collection of the deceased in a black plastic bag, fill the body with chemicals, and store it in a chilled container for weeks on end is not an end that befits our loved ones.

When will humanity recognise that we all desire to live and die in peace? We spend countless millions training people to kill and building bombs and missiles, and comparatively little teaching human beings about the nature of life and death.

Remember, too, those who died but did not leave a body to say goodbye to: those who drown at sea or go missing. Their families are left in a form of limbo. My neighbours recently suffered this fate when their beautiful adult daughter fell off a cliff and was swept out to sea. Despite many weeks of searching the coastline, no body was found.

Sometime afterwards, it was decided to have a church service to say goodbye to her, and it was one of the most powerful events I have ever attended. All of her family spoke with such love and affection in their hearts about their daughter and sister. The entire church could feel and share their pain and anguish, but the family had done all they could for her, said goodbye, and left her free. At the end, her sister recited the poem 'We Let You Go':

> *Into the darkness and warmth of the earth,*
> *we lay you down*
> *Into the sadness and smiles of our memories,*
> *we lay you down*
> *Into the cycle of living and dying and rising again,*
> *we lay you down*
> *May you rest in peace and fulfilment*
> *May you run straight home in God's embrace*
> *Into the freedom of wind and sunshine,*
> *we let you go*
> *Into the dance of stars and the planets,*
> *we let you go*
> *Into the wind's breath and the hands of the star*
> *maker, we let you go*
> *We love you, we miss you,*
> *we want you to be happy*
> *Go safely, go dancing, go running home.*

When I was twelve, my two grandmothers died within three months of each other. I was close to both of them. One of them lived near the national school that I attended, and every day after school I would visit her and help out with chores. My other grandmother lived in a nearby coastal town, and I would spend summer holidays at her house.

When they died, of a heart attack and cancer, I felt angry and sad. But the adults around me seemed to pay little or no attention to the feelings of a twelve-year-old. What did I know?

How a child views the world when faced with death is very different from how an adult does. Because children have not developed the full range of capacities to manage their emotions, it can be a frustrating time for them. Part of the education that society needs is to ensure we teach children how to face death and how it is part of the natural cycle of life. Young people are more resilient than we think, and rather than keep them in the dark about death, we need to open up their minds to it at an appropriate level that they can understand.

We often hear Christianity celebrate life after death, but I believe that we skip the important bit – the dying process. Perhaps we could introduce the meaning of death into our religion classes as part of the education curriculum, starting at junior level. We could make it part of the overall conversation and help children to understand it better. We would all benefit from this in the long run.

Finally, my own experience in dealing with death can be summarised as follows:

Do not be afraid to speak of the dead or to the dead! We need to remind ourselves of them regularly, as they have no voice. It is important that we recall good times and bad and not let them away from our memories for too long.

Listen to music and to the lyrics of songs that make you remember your loved ones. I have found that certain tunes, mainly ballads and slow sets, have stirred up huge waves of emotion in me. This has resulted in tears, but it is good to cry every now and then to let out the sadness. Some songs have particularly powerful words, such as 'Tears in Heaven' by Eric Clapton, who wrote it after the death of his four-year-old son Conor.

Seek professional help from counselling services. If you feel that your counsellor is not benefitting you, change to someone else. You need to find the right fit for you, as only you know what help you really need. Go with your gut on this one. If it doesn't feel right, then it probably isn't.

I will leave the final words to those who have left us and wait for us on the other side, as vocalised in the traditional Irish poem 'The Parting Glass':

> *But since it falls unto my lot*
> *That I should leave and you should not,*
> *I'll gently rise and I'll softly call,*
> *Goodnight, and joy be with you all.*

The End

9 781838 388904